Study Guide
for
The Armor of Light

MICHAEL CHRISTIAN

PARADISE • CALIFORNIA

Copyright © 2023 Michael Christian

All rights reserved.

ISBN 978-0-9894610-3-0

Library of Congress Control Number: 2023922919

Pronouns in Scripture that refer to the Father, Son, or Holy Spirit are captalized to honor Him.

Scripture quotations are taken from the *New King James Version*®. Copyright © 1982 by Thomas Nelson, Inc. Used by permission. All rights reserved.

Published by Twin Pillars Press
P. O. Box 531
Paradise, CA 95967

Visit https://michaelchristian.us

PRINTED IN THE UNITED STATES OF AMERICA

Contents

My Story iv
Introduction v

1. The Ultimate Showdown 1
2. God's Covenant of Protection 3
3. Living in the Light 5
4. Seeing into the Invisible Realm 7
5. Holy Angels, Your Heavenly Bodyguards 9
6. Standing Taller than Fallen Angels 12
7. Why You Must Pray 15
8. Walk by Faith, Not Sight 17
9. What Does It Mean to "Plead the Blood"? 19
10. The Spirit Leads Us to Dwell Safely 21
11. Wisdom Delivers from Trouble 23
12. What to Do Before the Battle 24
13. Abiding under the Shadow of the Almighty 25
14. Dwelling in the Secret Place of the Most High 27
15. Winning the Battle of the Tongue 29
16. The Covering of Your Local Church 31
17. A Balanced View of Spiritual Warfare 33
18. Is It God or the Devil? 35
19. How to Really Put On the Armor of Light 37
    Protection from Seven Kinds of Attack 42
    Review 43

My Story

Like most people, I accepted Christ to be forgiven and go to heaven when I died. I expected never to have another bad day. But within a few months, I was forced to come to a new conclusion—something evil was trying to destroy my life and relationships, and I was unprepared to deal with it. I had finally set my heart to do good, and I found that evil was present with me.[1]

My pastors called this spiritual warfare and explained that it happened to everyone, but I wouldn't say I liked the idea. I hadn't signed up for war, just salvation. As an untrained recruit thrust into battle, I had no training, no weapons, and little success. Honestly, I became angry with God. Since He created everything, why had He allowed evil into the world?[2] Why was I being attacked for living for God for once?[3] I wondered if I was a sacrificial pawn in a cruel cosmic chess match between God and the devil.[4]

For years after being saved, random thoughts bombarded me daily with reminders of my unsaved past, making me feel condemned and unworthy before God. Some days, I wondered if I had lost my salvation. Thankfully, others mentored and prayed me through these challenges.

In my desire to find answers, I longed for a Bible-based book like *The Armor of Light* to get up to speed more quickly, but I couldn't find it. However, the more I learned from the Word of God over the years, the better I dealt with the conflict until I got the upper hand.

Now, I'm happy to say that I have written *The Armor of Light,* the book I wished for as a new believer, hoping that what I learned will help you, too.

As you read, some things are simple to grasp, while others take longer to sink in. But as you meditate in God's Word and pray for wisdom, the Holy Spirit will give you understanding and victory over the unseen realm surrounding you.

The Armor of Light contains many footnotes to Scripture. I encourage you to look them up in your Bible and underline them if they speak to you. There is no substitute for reading the Bible for yourself.

Be sure to download the free Thank You Gift mentioned at the end of the book.

https://michaelchristian.us/armor-of-light-resources/

---

1 Romans 7:21
2 I didn't realize at the time that Adam and Eve made that choice, not God.
3 The enemy was pressuring me to quit living for God. It didn't work!
4 Jesus was the only One who sacrificed Himself for all.

Introduction

Jesus gave Paul the following instructions on the Damascus road.

"I will deliver you from the Jewish people, as well as from the Gentiles, to whom I now send you, *to open their eyes, to turn them from darkness to light, from the power of Satan to God*, that they may receive forgiveness of sins and an inheritance[5] among those who are sanctified by faith in Me." —Acts 26:17-18 (italics added)

Salvation is an eye-opening event in which we turn from worldly darkness to the light of Christ, from Satan to God. After that, our Christian life becomes an ongoing opening of our eyes to new truths from God's Word and stepping out of darkness into the light.

The Bible teaches about a *spiritual* dimension surrounding us. Every day in that arena, a spiritual war goes on between the forces of light and darkness, between God and the fallen angels who rebelled against His good and godly ways.

This war affects every area of your life, including your mind, will, emotions, self-image, dreams, marriage, children, parents, work, and relationships. We must acknowledge and face the reality of this conflict. Like it or not, it is what it is, and we can't change it. There's no place to run, hide, or remain neutral.

But we can rejoice in the great victory Jesus won for us on the cross. By accepting Jesus, we choose God's side, the winning side, become a victor in Him, and enjoy the blessings of God's protection, favor, and strength.

The Armor of Light will help open your eyes to unseen spiritual realities and show you how to live victoriously over invisible evils that affect you every day. You are engaged in a spiritual struggle, but the most effective form of spiritual warfare is focusing on Christ, not the dark side. You don't have to be an expert on evil to overcome it, but you need to love and trust Jesus. We win as we keep our eyes on and follow Him.

---

5 All the benefits of a restored relationship to God, including the Holy Spirit and His gifts.

CHAPTER 1

The Ultimate Showdown

One event is the basis for everything we do in Christianity: Jesus Christ defeated the devil by His death and resurrection and reconciled us to God by His blood. After dying, Jesus descended into hell, took from the enemy the keys of death and Hades, and released from their cells the souls of the righteous dead (who looked forward to His coming).

He then led a triumphant victory procession from the underworld into the third heaven. Because of His shed blood, the gates of the kingdom of heaven opened wide for believers for the first time. By His cross, Jesus restored what humanity had lost: our *relationship* with God and our *authority* under God.

Review Questions

1. What is a champion, as understood in this chapter? Does a champion fight for himself or others? (p. 1)

2. By obedience unto death, Jesus earned the name above every name, and His name has authority over which three realms (see Philippians 2:10)? (pp. 2-3)

3. When God records your name in the Lamb's Book of Life, what official right is granted to you? (p. 3)

4. All authority in heaven and earth belongs to Jesus. (Matthew 28:18) Since He has "all authority," how much does that leave the devil? According to this verse, has God "authorized" or given the devil "permission" to do anything? (p. 4)

5. Does being raised up and seated with Christ in heavenly places give you more or less authority? Why? (pp. 4-5)

6. Jesus gave the church the keys of the kingdom of heaven, which includes the right to bind and loose. (Matthew 16:18-19) According to Jesus' instructions, who does the binding, Jesus or us? How do we bind the demons that come against us, and in whose name? (pp. 6-7)

7. How can we use the keys of the kingdom of heaven to purify our spiritual atmospheres? What is the advantage of doing this? (pp. 7-8)

8. Who is responsible for dealing with the devil, God or us? What does it mean to operate in partnership with God? (p. 9)

9. As a royal priesthood, what are we privileged to do? (p. 10)

Secret #1

Having defeated Satan decisively and eternally, Jesus gave you who believe the authority to command evil spirits to depart from you and your family in His matchless name!

CHAPTER 2

God's Covenant of Protection

God placed Adam and Eve in the Garden of Eden to tend and keep it (or guard it). Made in the image of God and full of His glory, they were the original *guardians* of the planet. They had a close relationship with God, exercised His authority as the under-rulers of earth, and had His Word to guide them. ("Don't eat of the fruit.") God made them no promise of protection because *they* were the protectors. It was not until after they fell that people needed protection from the enemy.

Review Questions

1. Which great man of God received the Bible's first direct promise of protection? What three things did God promise him? (pp. 11-13)

   _____
   _____
   _____

2. What makes a blood covenant ceremony so special? What do covenant makers pledge as the guarantee of the covenant? What modern relationship is a covenant and not a contract? (p. 14-15)

   _____
   _____
   _____

3. Which Scriptures tell us that the blessing of Abraham comes on non-Jewish believers? (p. 15)

   _____
   _____
   _____

4. The blessing of Abraham came fully on Jesus Christ and those who are in Him. That blessing includes promises of protection. Of the verses listed, which are the most meaningful to you? Why? (pp. 16-17)

   _____
   _____
   _____

5. Protection is a covenant blessing. What steps can any person take to enter God's covenant of protection? (pp. 18-20)

_____
_____
_____

Secret #2

To walk in divine protection, you must make a covenant with God through faith in Jesus Christ, through which you receive forgiveness of sins, right standing with God, peace, protection, and eternal reward. You enter the covenant when you personally invite Jesus to be your Savior and Lord.

CHAPTER 3

Living in the Light

We put on the armor of light as we turn from worldly darkness to the light of the Bible. In our pre-Christian life, the world indoctrinated us into its philosophies. But now, God's Word is a lamp to our feet and a light to our path. Christian enlightenment comes as we fill our minds with the pure truth of God's Word. God's light overcomes deception, ignorance, and confusion, just as the glow of a tiny candle dispels the thickest darkness.

Review Questions

1. How does our new birth parallel the original creation? (pp. 21-22)

2. What happens when we worship Him, who is light? (pp. 22-23)

3. When you were born again, what part of your being did God re-create? Which parts of your being did He not transform? What happens when we have an illuminated spirit and a darkened soul? (p. 23)

4. What choices must we make to live in the light? (pp. 24-25)

5. What is the secret of spiritual transformation? (pp. 25-26)

6. Since beliefs control actions, what's the best way to change our behavior? (pp. 26-27)

7. How does the metamorphosis of a butterfly illustrate spiritual transformation? (pp. 27-28)

8. Has the Word of God changed your identity, your estimatation of who you are? What difference has this made in your life? (pp. 28-29)

SECRET #3

God refathered your spirit when you said Yes to Jesus, but you must allow the brilliant light of His Word to enter your soul, renew your mind, and scatter the worldly darkness. As you plant the new thoughts of God's Word in your heart, your beliefs and behavior change. You acquire the mind of Christ and radiate His love by living and walking in the light of your new identity.

CHAPTER 4

Seeing into the Invisible Realm

In the beginning, God created the heavens (plural) and the earth, establishing a divine order in creation. The Bible word "heaven" is confusing because it refers to three distinct realms. Jesus, however, promised to instruct us in the mysteries of the kingdom of heaven so that we can understand the natural and spiritual worlds.

Review Questions

1. What are the two aspects of creation? (pp. 30-31)

   _____
   _____
   _____

2. Which did God create first? Which part depends on the other? Which part of creation is permanent, the seen or the unseen? (pp. 31-32)

   _____
   _____
   _____

3. Describe the three heavens of the Bible. Where do believers go when they die? In which heaven is God's throne? Where does spiritual warfare take place? Which heaven makes up sky and space? (pp. 32-35)

   _____
   _____
   _____

4. Jesus declared His disciples would understand the mysteries of the kingdom of heaven. The kingdom of heaven is the supreme spiritual realm, also called the kingdom of God. So, what did Jesus mean when He said that the "kingdom of heaven" was at hand? (Matthew, writing to the Jews, preferred the phrase kingdom of heaven, while Mark and Luke, writing to Gentiles, used "kingdom of God" in parallel accounts.) (pp. 35-36)

   _____
   _____
   _____

5. Why did our Master Teacher, the wisest, kindest Man ever to live, think it necessary to talk about the devil? (pp. 35-36)

_____
_____
_____

6. Modern travel and medicine, space exploration, computers, and personal, wireless communications are incredible breakthroughs compared to the technology of one hundred years ago. As impressive as science and technology are, what shocking limitations do they have? Identify some problems rooted in the spiritual realm that cannot be solved by technology and natural, human solutions? (pp. 36-37)

_____
_____
_____

SECRET #4

A spiritual environment surrounds you. Between God's heaven and earth lies a second heaven, where angels and demons contend for the souls of men. For this reason, natural solutions can't fix problems rooted in the spiritual realm. But in Christ, the kingdom of heaven—the third heaven—gives you authority and power over everything that fights against you in the second heaven.

CHAPTER 5

Holy Angels, Your Heavenly Bodyguards

Humanity has always been fascinated by angels. The Bible refers to powerful, holy angels of varying ranks and commissions. Primarily, they aid people in achieving God's purposes. However, a careful study of the biblical records reveals that angels did *not* always help men. For this reason, we should pay special attention to the first recorded instances where angels assisted human beings and understand why they suddenly came alongside. We can benefit from their ministry when we realize what made their assistance possible.

Review Questions

1. Can you name different kinds of angels based on their functions? What fraction of the angels fell from grace to follow Satan, and how many remained loyal to God? (pp. 38-39)

   _____
   _____
   _____

2. At which point in human history does the devil's influence appear unrestrained? Which two books of the Bible touch on the first 2,000 years of Earth's history?[6] (p. 39)

   _____
   _____
   _____

3. Job was a Gentile who lived before Abraham and was not a partaker of the Abrahamic covenant. Did he have a covenant with God or any promise of protection from God? In the book of Job, angels are called "angels," "holy ones," "morning stars," and "sons of God." Does the Bible record them helping Job in his affliction? Did the "watchers" assist King Nebuchadnezzar, a Gentile king? (Daniel 4:13, 17, 23) (p. 40)

   _____
   _____
   _____

4. Which Bible chapter contains the first reference to holy angels helping people? Which chapter first

---

6 The customs recorded in the book of Job point to the patriarchal period prior to the covenant God made with Abraham. Neither Job nor his friends quoted Scripture. He probably lived approximately 2,000 B.C.

records God making a blood covenant with man? Do you think there is a connection between the two? Can you describe the vision that Abraham's grandson Jacob received regarding the ministry of angels? What does it mean? (p. 40-41)

_____
_____
_____

5. What did Jesus promise Nathaniel that he would see? The angels of God would be ascending and descending upon whom? Where does Scripture describe a connection between faith in Jesus and receiving the ministry of angels? Does the New Testament record more or less angelic activity than the Old Testament? (p. 41-43)

_____
_____
_____

6. How does Psalm 91 describe the ministry of angels? According to the book of Revelation, how many angels will it take to bind Satan? (p. 43-44)

_____
_____
_____

7. According to Psalm 103:20, angels listen for God's Word to perform it. What do you think happens when the angels hear God's Word coming from your mouth? What do the angels do when your words contradict God's Word? Is it any less God's Word when *you* speak it? (p. 44-45)

_____
_____
_____

8. How would you describe the "Double Camp"? Have you ever been aware, like Jacob or Elisha, that the angelic forces of God surrounded you? (p. 45)

_____
_____
_____

9. Jesus referred to the angels of little children who always saw the face of God, but He was speaking of Jewish children, circumcised into the covenant of Abraham and dedicated to God in the temple. Might there be a link between presenting or dedicating a child to God and the protective ministry of guardian angels? (p 46-47)

_____
_____
_____

10. According to Hebrews 1:14, angels are ministering spirits sent forth to minister for whom? Can angels override our free will choices? Are we to worship angels? How might angels help at the moment of our death? (p. 47-49)

___

Secret #5

Powerful angels camp around you. They protect, help, and deliver you in ways you don't always see. God's angels guard you day and night, and you release them to do their jobs when you confess Jesus as Lord, pray, and speak faith-filled words.

CHAPTER 6

Standing Taller than Fallen Angels

No one is greater or more powerful than God. He created the whole creation to serve Him, and He is worthy of all our worship. However, one of God's created beings, an angel, rebelled against Him and wanted to be worshiped instead of God. As a result, the Lord expelled him from heaven along with the angels who followed him. God stripped them of their heavenly powers as they fell. Jesus defeated these fallen angels through His cross, resurrection, descent into hell, and glorious ascension.

Review Questions

1. The devil fell through pride in the abilities and talents God gave to him. How do we keep ourselves from falling in the same way? (p. 51)

   _____
   _____
   _____

2. What kinds of problems do demons cause on earth? (pp. 51-52)

   _____
   _____
   _____

3. Jesus overcame the devil. Now, Jesus lives in you. Which verse declares that He who is in you is greater than he who is in the world? (p. 52)

   _____
   _____
   _____

4. Should Christians be afraid of the devil? Why or why not? (p. 53)

   _____
   _____
   _____

5. Can you trust what the devil says? What did Jesus say about him? (p. 53)

   _____

6. What is the enemy's greatest weapon? What is our best protection against it? (pp. 53-54)

7. Which three attributes does God possess that the enemy lacks? (p. 54)

8. Demons do not die like people. What advantage does that give them over the generations of human families? (pp. 54-55)

9. After which event did God permanently terminate Satan's access to His presence? Where does Scripture record this? As a result, God has no conversations with the devil about you, nor does He give him permission to attack you. The "accuser of the brethren" can no longer accuse you before God because he has been ejected from God's courtroom. (pp. 55-56)

10. After years of persecution, the apostle Paul discovered that he was not fighting against flesh and blood, but something else. What was it? (p. 56)

11. Does the devil have power over your freedom to choose? Should you blame him for your bad choices? (p. 56)

12. What are principalities, powers, rulers of the darkness of this age, and spiritual hosts of wickedness in heavenly places? Have you noticed signs of these at work in your community? (pp. 57-58)

13. How do we combat spiritual resistance? (pp. 58-59)

14. What spiritual forces operate in the second heaven? Which forces for good are present to help and protect you? (pp. 59-61)

SECRET #6

The devil is a fallen angel and not in the God class. Unlike God, he is in one place at a time, lost power when he was thrown out of God's presence, and doesn't know God's plans. The Lord and His angels protect you and fight for you in the second heaven.

CHAPTER 7

Why You Must Pray

We all know we should pray more, but the question is, why? If the sovereign God controls all things, what difference do our little prayers make? Jesus, however, did not look at prayer that way. We learn from Him that prayer is essential because He practiced it daily and encouraged us to do so. Until we understand that our prayers determine how much divine intervention happens in our lives, we will continue to pray weak and sporadic prayers. But when we realize that God depends on us to pray *before* He can move, our prayers become raw, honest, and intense. Fulfilling your divine destiny depends on your *prayerfulness*.

Review Questions

1. Which fundamental principle of prayer does the book of James record? What did Jesus say about prayer? (p. 63)

2. In the beginning, God gave man dominion. What does dominion mean? Was free will included in the dominion? (pp. 63-64)

3. After God gave man dominion, why could He not overrule man's choices? If God acts in a way that contradicts His spoken Word, would that make Him a liar? Can God lie? Does God's own Word place limits on His sovereignty? Why is God's Word as sovereign as He is? Which Old Testament account illustrates the unchangeable power of a decree? (pp. 64-66)

4. After God put man in charge of the earth, who had to initiate everything done on earth? Why can't the Lord intervene until a man or woman asks? When people overlook this simple truth, they wait for the Lord to move while He waits for them to do what? (pp. 66-67)

5. Christians often say, "God is in control," but that phrase is not in the Bible. Instead, the Bible says, "The Lord reigns." Imagine a king reigning with full authority over a country. Does he control (micromanage) everything that goes on in it? But isn't he still the ultimate authority to whom all are accountable? Could God control everything that happens on the planet after He gave man dominion without contradicting His Word? (pp. 67-69)

6. When we partner with God in prayer, the coming together of which two things produces amazing results? How do we know Jesus' beliefs about prayer? (pp. 70-72)

7. Why does God seek out intercessors? (pp. 72-73)

8. How do we put our prayers "on the record"? (pp. 73-74)

SECRET #7

God's kingdom comes and His will is done only when man prays. To receive divine intervention, you must exercise your free will and ask for God's amazing help in Jesus' name.

CHAPTER 8

Walk by Faith, Not Sight

King David was a warrior who survived many battles and life-threatening events. This man after God's own heart had great faith in the protective power of God and wrote about it. So, what does it mean to have faith in God?

Review Questions

1. Which of the Scriptures listed is your favorite? Why? (pp. 75-77)
   _____
   _____
   _____

2. What is a simple definition of faith? Was Abraham's faith a blind faith? God accounts faith in His people as the equivalent of _____? Why? How does the Bible define faith in Hebrews 11:1? (pp. 77-78)
   _____
   _____
   _____

3. Since faith is so important, how do we increase our faith? Does faith come instantaneously or as a process? How can we grow our faith? (pp. 78-79)
   _____
   _____
   _____

4. Can you name the two components of faith? How do they work together and reinforce each other? (p. 79)
   _____
   _____
   _____

SECRET #8

Once you have prayed, you must stand firm in faith and patience, trusting God's revealed Word and His faithful lovingkindness to bring His Word to pass.

CHAPTER 9

What Does It Mean to "Plead the Blood"?

As a young Christian, I heard older Christians speak of the protective power of the blood of Christ. They would say, "I plead the blood." I assumed this phrase was somewhere in the Bible, but I couldn't find it. So, I questioned God if this was a biblical concept. If it was, I wanted to know how to "plead the blood" in prayers of protection. The blood of Christ is one of the great weapons of our warfare because it procured our forgiveness and right standing with God.

Review Questions

1. How does the story of the father and his teenage son involved in the car accident illustrate God's love? (pp. 80-81)

   _____
   _____
   _____

2. Name some of the benefits of the blood of Jesus. (pp. 81-82)

   _____
   _____
   _____

3. Have you ever heard the phrase "pleading the blood"? What does the word plead mean? How can we use the blood of Christ as evidence for acquittal in the courtroom of God? (pp. 82-84)

   _____
   _____
   _____

4. What is the highest form of intercessory prayer? Have you ever entered the courtroom of God as a priest presenting the evidence of the blood of Christ on behalf of another? Is that something you are willing to do? (pp. 84-85)

   _____
   _____
   _____

5. Which Old Testament ceremony required believers to apply the blood of a lamb to the doorposts of their houses? What effect did the presence of the blood have? Since Jesus is our Passover lamb, how can we apply His blood to our homes and lives? (pp. 85-87)

___
___
___

SECRET #9

When you plead the blood of Christ in intercession, God sends the Holy Spirit to lead the one for whom you pray to repentance and faith in Christ, that they may receive forgiveness of sins and the power to go and sin no more. When you apply the Passover blood, you create a "bloodline" of protection around those you love.

CHAPTER 10

The Spirit Leads Us to Dwell Safely

Terrorism and random violence have become common in our country in recent years. As we pray for safety, we should ask ourselves *how* God will answer our prayers. How does He keep His people safe in dangerous situations? The Bible gives us several examples.

Review Questions

1. Which do you think is easier for God to do? (1) Stop rebellious people from doing evil? (2) Move His children out of harm's way? Why? Does the story of Cain and Abel shed light on this question? How did God handle Cain's evil intent? (See the footnote. p. 88)

   _____
   _____
   _____

2. How does God lead his children away from dangerous people and situations? How does God reveal inside information to His children? Which gift of the Spirit describes this manifestation? (p. 89)

   _____
   _____
   _____

3. Give examples of how God warned people in the Bible and modern times. (pp. 89-90)

   _____
   _____
   _____

4. While it's possible people may give you prophetic words of warning, who is the main person God speaks to about your life? What can you do to hear God better? How can you practice being led by the Spirit? (pp. 90-91)

   _____
   _____
   _____

SECRET #10

Allow yourself to be guided out of harm's way by the promptings of the Holy Spirit. Stay in tune by abiding in the secret place with the Lord, watching, praying, listening, and obeying.

CHAPTER 11

Wisdom Delivers from Trouble

God created the earth through wisdom, and we need it to build our lives. (Proverbs 3:19) Walking in wisdom is a key to living in divine protection. The book of Proverbs personifies wisdom as a woman crying out warnings to avoid the people, places, and practices that get us into trouble. (Proverbs 1:20)

Review Questions

1. One proverb says, "If a bird sees a trap being set, it knows to stay away." (Proverbs 1:17, NLT) What are some reasons people fail to see the traps set before them? (pp. 92-93)

   _____
   _____
   _____

2. How does a person obtain wisdom? What does the Bible say about this? (pp. 93-94)

   _____
   _____
   _____

3. Who do you trust to speak wisdom into your life? Is their wisdom Bible-based? (p. 94)

   _____
   _____
   _____

SECRET #11

Wisdom is a key to divine safety, but foolishness opens you to trouble and sorrow. Make wisdom your friend and associate with wise people, and you will become wise.

CHAPTER 12

What to Do Before the Battle

In one Old Testament battle, King Jehoshaphat placed singers and praisers at the front of the army as they went to war. It sounded ridiculous! But according to Scripture, God *leads* His troops into battle. So, the best place for the singers was at the front of the army near God. The presence of the Lord so unnerved the enemy armies that they fought among themselves and fled before Israel arrived. Prayer and songs of praise won the battle before Israel shot an arrow.

Review Questions

1. Can you think of a way to apply this principle daily? (pp. 95-96)

   _____
   _____
   _____

2. Name two instances when Jesus prayed before going into a situation. (pp. 96-97)

   _____
   _____
   _____

3. Is God surprised by the unforeseen circumstances that catch you off guard? If He knows what will happen beforehand, you can trust that He made provision for you. Your job is to seek and find what He has provided. (p. 97)

   _____
   _____
   _____

SECRET #12

Pray and praise on your way to the battle, knowing the Lord goes in front of you, prepares the way before you, and fights the battle for you.

CHAPTER 13

Abiding under the Shadow of the Almighty

David came to King Saul as a young shepherd boy seeking permission to fight Goliath. He told the king how he had fought a lion and a bear while protecting his father's sheep. Then, he predicted that the giant Goliath would become like one of them, seeing that he had defied the armies of the living God.

Review Questions

1. What was the secret of David's faith in this situation? What did he and Israel have that Goliath did not have? (p. 99)

   _____
   _____
   _____

2. Which Bible passage is best known worldwide? Why do you think that is? (p. 99)

   _____
   _____
   _____

3. Which promise did God make to Abraham that David believed with all his heart? Was that promise in effect in the days of King Hezekiah? Is it still in effect over Israel today? (pp. 12, 99-102)

   _____
   _____
   _____

4. Which Psalm outlines the wonderful protections belonging to those in covenant with the Lord? Which of its promises means the most to you today? (pp. 102-104)

   _____
   _____
   _____

5. In which Old Testament events did the Lord demonstrate the power of His protection? How might this apply to us today? (pp. 104-105)

   _____

SECRET #13

When you make time to dwell in the secret place of the Most High, you abide under the shadow of the Almighty. As He did for David and Israel, God covers you and your family with the shield of His presence.

CHAPTER 14

Dwelling in the Secret Place of the Most High

As a child, I loved hiding in a fort made of blankets or in a thicket of trees. Psalm 91 describes the "secret place of the Most High" as a fort-like covering of God's presence. God's secret place is the ultimate place of protection. He is our refuge, fortress, and hiding place.

Review Questions

1. Which of the Scriptures that describe God's secret place, hiding place, or refuge is your favorite? Why? (pp. 106-107)

   _____
   _____
   _____

2. How can imperfect people dwell in the secret place of the Most High with One who is holy? What is the difference between Christianity and religious systems based on human works? Why isn't it possible for a person living under a "works" system to experience true peace? (pp. 108-109)

   _____
   _____
   _____

3. Is the administrator of the new covenant faith or law? Why is the law no longer the administrator? (pp. 109-110)

   _____
   _____
   _____

4. If our access to the secret place is based on Christ's sacrifice, is there any limit to the Psalm 91 protection we can receive? How do we make a "secret place" in daily life? (pp. 110-111)

   _____
   _____
   _____

5. Mary became pregnant with Jesus when the Holy Spirit overshadowed her with His presence. As we spend time in the secret place with God, what kinds of things might we become pregnant with by the Holy Spirit? (p. 111)

_____
_____
_____

SECRET #14

Remember, access to the secret place of the Most High is not for those whose works are perfect, but for you who have been made righteous by faith in Jesus' blood. As you abide under the shadow of the Lord's wings, His fortress of protection shelters you.

CHAPTER 15

Winning the Battle of the Tongue

Christians often request prayer for the "spiritual warfare" they are going through. But in many cases, the stress may be self-inflicted. My tongue used to get me in trouble, which I then blamed on a spiritual attack. But honestly, I lacked self-control. Admittedly, it is a struggle to learn to speak patiently, kindly, and wisely, but by so doing, we offend fewer people, producing a less stressful life.

Review Questions

1. Does the dream described in the first part of this chapter make sense to you? Have you ever been aware of external forces influencing what you say? (pp. 112-113)

2. Why does the Bible state that the tongue can be "set on fire by hell"? How are death and life in the power of the tongue? Have others' words left scars in your soul? (pp. 113-114)

3. What kinds of things can we do to put a muzzle on our mouths, figuratively speaking? Does it help you to imagine the Lord putting a bridle in your mouth and holding the reins? (James 1:26) (pp. 114-116)

4. Blessing and cursing should not proceed from the same mouth. How can we stop the negative talk that comes out of our mouths? (pp. 116-117)

5. Those who "prophesy" under the inspiration of the Holy Spirit speak edification, exhortation,

and comfort to people. What do those three words mean? People who are beaten down by the world and their consciences mostly need _____. (pp. 117-118)

_____
_____
_____

6. What is the difference between being an accuser and an intercessor? (p. 118)

_____
_____
_____

7. Why is changing our behavior more meaningful to others than saying "I'm sorry"? (p. 119)

_____
_____
_____

8. Pray the prayer to cancel the power of toxic words spoken over you. From now on, believe what God's Word says about you more than what dysfunctional human beings have said about you. (p. 119)

_____
_____
_____

9. Pray the prayer to cancel the harmful words you have spoken over others. Resolve in your heart to be slow to speak and kind. Take a moment, pause, and pray for the right words and tone before you say anything. (pp. 119-120)

_____
_____
_____

SECRET #15

Learn to control your tongue. A tongue that encourages and builds up people, that speaks life, love, grace, forgiveness, and comfort will be blessed.

CHAPTER 16

The Covering of Your Local Church

Sometimes, people say, "I don't believe in the organized church." I'm afraid I have to disagree for one fundamental reason. Jesus Christ is the One who organized it and brought it into being. He said, "On this rock I will build my church, and the gates of Hades shall not prevail against it." (Matthew 16:18) If the idea of the church is good enough for Jesus, then it's good enough for me. There is strength and protection in belonging to a local church, and the gates of hell shall not prevail against it.

Review Questions

1. What is the solid rock confession upon which Christ builds His church? (pp. 121-122)

2. What does it mean to have an "open heaven" over a worshiping church? According to Isaiah 4:5-6, God's glory rests above His assemblies, including the church. Over all the glory, there is a covering. What benefits belong to those under the covering? What is the overarching promise of church life? (pp. 122-123)

3. What can we learn from Pastor Steve Grandy's dream? (pp. 123-124)

4. A mighty angel accompanied the congregation of Israel in the wilderness, and God assigns angels to cover and protect local churches. (Cp. Rev. 1:20, 2:1, etc.) Why are churches uncommon? As a local church member, you are joined with the prayers of all the intercessors who have prayed for the church. Are you possibly the answer to their prayers? (pp. 124-125)

5. How did the Roman centurion understand the authority of Jesus? (Matt. 8:8) How did his perception give him great faith? Do you think he saw Jesus as the General of a spiritual army? As a military man, the centurion gave orders to the men under him and submitted to those over him. What would have happened to the centurion if he stopped obeying those over him? Do you think spiritual authority operates similarly? (pp. 125-126)

_____
_____
_____

6. According to Ephesians 4:11, the office of pastor was ordained by God. Why is it important to respect the God-ordained office, even though imperfect men occupy it? What should we do if someone in authority hurts us? (pp. 126-127)

_____
_____
_____

7. Jesus said that a house divided cannot stand. Why is division in a church so devastating? What happens to a church's anointing of the Holy Spirit when the church is divided rather than united? (Psalm 133:1-3. The oil in this verse refers to the anointing oil poured on the priest's head at his consecration.) (p. 127)

_____
_____
_____

8. When we tithe to our local church, God promises to "rebuke the devourer" for our sake. (Malachi 3:8-12) By "rebuking the devourer," God extends His covering of protection over our possessions and work, minimizing our losses, so we are blessed. When we tithe today, whom are we honoring? (p. 128)

_____
_____
_____

SECRET #16

Do not forsake going to church, for it provides a spiritual covering against which the gates of hell cannot prevail. Submit to the spiritual authority over you and refrain from causing division, a sin that weakens the church.

CHAPTER 17

A Balanced View of Spiritual Warfare

Jesus did not ignore the spiritual realm as though it did not exist. But some people are obsessed with the spirit world and cast evil spirits out of everything. Jesus did not do that either. So, what should be our approach?

Review Questions

1. How can we tell when we are under spiritual attack? (pp. 129-130)

2. What are some things we can do to fight back? Which of these works best for you?

3. What does it mean to "downshift" during a time of spiritual warfare? (pp. 130-131)

4. What can delay our answer to prayer? What do we do if there is a delay? (pp. 131-132)

5. Which two main thoughts guide us during a season of spiritual warfare? What important principle do we learn from Peter walking on the water? (p. 132)

6. Sometimes, we obsess about the darkness, but what is more helpful? Which Old Testament verse identifies our inward lamp? Name some things we can do to make our spirit shine with the glory of God so that it repels the darkness. Which ones work best for you? (pp. 132-133)

   _____
   _____
   _____

7. In summary, what two things should we do when things are dark? (p. 133)

   _____
   _____
   _____

SECRET #17

Recognize when you are under attack and downshift into warfare mode. Don't isolate yourself but spend more time with God and His people. Keep your eyes on Jesus and your spirit burning with His Word and Holy Spirit.

CHAPTER 18

Is It God or the Devil?

In this present age, both God and the devil, good and evil, are present in the earth, contending for the souls of men. God tells us in His Word to submit to Him and resist the devil, and the enemy will flee from us. But what things do we resist? And what do we accept as coming from the hand of God? How can we tell what is of God and what is of the devil?

Review Questions

1. What should our proper attitude toward evil be? What is the first step we should take in resisting the enemy? Who is the true Lion in the spirit realm? If you were the enemy, what kind of person would you attack? What kind of person would you avoid? (pp. 134-135)

   _____
   _____
   _____

2. In what area of life should we begin resisting the devil? (pp. 135-136)

   _____
   _____
   _____

3. Which saying of Jesus helps us discern the hand of God from the hand of the devil? Did Jesus ever permit demons to afflict people to teach them spiritual lessons? Who gave the devil permission to attack the human race? (pp. 136-137)

   _____
   _____
   _____

4. Does God believe that the end justifies the means? Does God use the devil to teach His children lessons? Why or why not? What means does God use to accomplish His righteous purposes? (pp. 137-138)

   _____
   _____
   _____

5. What does the law of sowing and reaping state? According to this law, can a person use unrighteous means to accomplish a righteous goal? Why would it be counterproductive for God to use the devil to teach His children spiritual lessons? (p. 138)

___

6. What is the "chastening of the Lord" described in Scripture? What is God's agent of correction? If *all* authority in heaven and earth belongs to Jesus, then the devil has *no* authority. If he has *no* authority, can he have *any* sanction or permission from God to do anything? (pp. 138-139)

___

7. What is the devil's favorite trap? (p. 139)

___

8. Does God send sickness to correct His people? Why is it important to discern disease and infirmity as the work of the thief? (pp. 139-140)

___

9. Does God put cancer on people? How do we know? (pp. 140-141)

___

10. Are acts of nature acts of God? Have you ever used your authority in Christ to speak to storms, wind, and waves and command them to be still? (p. 141)

___

SECRET #18

Submit to God and resist the devil in every way he comes against you. Don't simply endure evil but resist it until it flees from you in terror! Don't blame God for the works of the thief. God is not your problem, but your ally and Savior in times of trouble.

CHAPTER 19

How to Really Put On the Armor of Light

The armor of God passage in Ephesians 6:10-18 is an eye-opener. It speaks of the spiritual struggle we call spiritual warfare and instructs us in how to succeed in it. These verses describe spiritual armor that protects us from the wiles of the enemy. Given by God's grace, this armor enables us to stand victoriously against attack and take new ground for Jesus.

God gives us the armor, but our job is to put it on and learn to use it. The Bible gives few details about how to put it on, and there is more than one way to look at it. In 2 Corinthians 10:4, Paul tells us that *"the weapons of our warfare are not carnal* [or fleshly] *but mighty in God."* Our weapons are not of this world.

Most teachings on the armor of God go into detail about historical Roman armor and its parallels to spiritual warfare. However, I've come to believe that Roman gear is merely an illustration of the real thing. The armor of this world is external and physical, but the armor of God is internal and spiritual. Paul explained in Romans 13:12 that spiritual armor is the armor of light. It comes from renewing our minds in seven key concepts.

Take, for example, the breastplate of righteousness. We are to put on righteousness as our breastplate. The active element in the armor is righteousness, not an invisible, breastplate-shaped object dropped on us from heaven. It's a concept we believe and understand. Through faith, we have received the free gift of Christ's righteousness. Our right standing with God does not depend on our flawed performance but on the perfect righteousness lived by Jesus. The covering of Christ's righteousness functions like a breastplate, protecting our spiritual heart from condemnation. It ensures we can hold our heads up and pray to God for help when we need it most—when our righteousness fails and we feel the most unworthy.

We put on each part of the armor by learning the revelation or the lesson taught by that piece.

Review Questions

1. Have you ever been confused about putting on and using the armor of God? (pp. 142-143)

   _____
   _____
   _____

2. What is the first reference in the Bible to a piece of armor? How does Psalm 91:4 describe truth? Where does Paul call the armor of God "the armor of light"? (p. 143)

   _____
   _____

3. In Ephesians 6:10-13, why does Paul tell the church to put on the whole armor of God? (See v. 11) What does he mean when he says, "For we do not wrestle against flesh and blood"? Who, then, do we wrestle against? (See v. 13). (p. 144)

4. How did you put on the armor of God? Have you ever visualized or confessed putting on each piece of the armor in prayer? How well did the armor protect you? Did you experience consistent results? (pp. 145-146)

5. Have you ever considered putting on the armor by receiving the revelation (or the lesson) of each piece? Paul listed seven things we must understand to put on the armor. What are they? (pp. 146-147)

6. How do I put on truth like a belt? What does it protect me from? Why must my source of truth be external to myself? How is God's Word like a compass? (pp. 147-148)

7. How do I put on righteousness as a breastplate? What part of my being does it protect? What does it protect me from? Do I put on the breastplate by doing righteous deeds? (p. 149)

8. If the breastplate of righteousness depends on my righteousness, what happens to my breastplate when I sin? Has sin ever made you feel condemned and cut off from the help of God? Can my imperfect human righteousness protect me when I fail? What can? What is the righteousness of faith? Whose righteousness is it based on? How do I receive it? Do you suppose the breastplate could have two layers? What are they? (pp. 149-153)

9. According to Romans 5:1, we were justified (or declared righteous) by faith in Jesus. Justification gives us _____ with God because He has forgiven our sins. We receive that peace when we put on the breastplate of trusting in Christ's righteousness, not our works. What emotions do God's grace and forgiveness produce in you? Are you thankful for what Jesus did? Has this impacted your desire to serve God? Did the gospel of peace transform your willingness to yield to, obey, and submit to the Lord? (pp. 153-154)

10. The Amplified version of Ephesians 6:15 reads, "And having shod your feet in preparation [to face the enemy with the firm footed stability, the promptness, and *the readiness produced by* the good news] of the gospel of peace." According to Scripture, our feet are shod with *readiness* produced by the gospel of peace. Can you see that the battle sandals you put on are shoes of readiness? (p. 154)

11. What do shoes and feet symbolize? Are you willing to say, "Lord, not my will, but Yours be done"? Are you willing to surrender to God and allow Him to direct your path? If so, you are *ready* to serve Him. You have your battle sandals on when you are yielded to the Lord and desire His will above your own. But what happens to your shoes and feet if you return to doing your own will? (p. 154)

12. The enemy attacks us daily with "flaming arrows" or "fiery darts." These troubling thoughts are shot into our minds and burn with fear, doubt, anger, discouragement, depression, guilt, unworthiness, etc. These thoughts are not your thoughts and originate outside of yourself. Have you ever had a weird, totally bizarre, or ugly thought and wondered if you were going crazy? Is it a relief to know these are not your thoughts but have been projected into your mind by the enemy? (p. 155)

13. You can quench or extinguish these flaming arrows by taking up faith in God's Word like a shield. First, you must become consciously aware of the fiery thoughts when they come. Then, identify the area of concern the thought stirs up and find the Bible's promises that speak to that issue. You have to believe God's promise *more* than the fear or worry. Hold the promise like a shield between you and the flaming arrows, repeating it as often as needed. (p. 155)

14. Do you have a written list of God's promises covering your most common fears and concerns? How can you hold the promise closer than the problem? Learning to use a physical shield requires training, and it will take practice to calm your thoughts and emotions by believing God's promises.

15. How does 1 Thessalonians 5:8 help define the helmet of salvation? How does the Greek definition of *hope* differ from our modern concept? How does your attitude change by strapping on the helmet? Though you have all the other armor pieces, what happens if you don't have on the helmet? What modern-day examples show what it is like to wear the helmet? The helmet of salvation protects us from what kinds of attitudes? (pp. 155-158)

16. We must take "the sword of the Spirit, which is the Word of God." What is the original Greek word for "word" in this verse? Does it refer to the written Word or a spoken Word? Why is it important to declare the Word of God aloud? When did Jesus demonstrate using the sword of the Spirit? Is the sword a defensive or offensive weapon, or both? (pp. 158-160)

17. Every Roman soldier carried a spear, but the spear is not named in Ephesians 6. However, Paul told us to put on the "whole armor" of God. To be fully equipped, we also need a spear to strike the enemy at a distance. What spiritual spear is mentioned in Ephesians 6:18? How is prayer like throwing a spear? Roman soldiers had many lances and spears to choose from, so name some different kinds of prayers we can pray. Is prayer limited by distance, or can it be hurled a long way like a spear? (pp.160-162)

SECRET #19

Put on the full "armor of light." As you receive the revelation of each piece, you are protected from the lies, deceptions, discouragement, and flaming arrows of the enemy. Be encouraged! You are an overcomer because the Spirit of Jesus Christ, the Champion, lives in you.

Protection from Seven Kinds of Attack

1. *Truth* protects you from the *deception* of worldly philosophies, demonic lies, and half-truths that abound in the culture and contradict the Bible. It protects you from every high thing that exalts itself against the knowledge of God and His Word. (2 Corinthians 10:5)

2. Your *righteousness* (right standing before God through faith in Jesus) gives you confidence in God. It protects you from *feelings of unworthiness and shame* caused by the enemy's voice of *accusation* and *condemnation*. Such feelings may keep you from praying when you need God's help the most, such as after a failure when you are most tempted to give up.

3. The shoes of *readiness* guide your feet from the *path of self-will* onto the path of God's will.

4. *Faith* in God's promises protects your mind and emotions from *the obsessive fire of disruptive thoughts,* such as fear, worry, discouragement, depression, despair, anger, lust, jealousy, pride, selfish ambition, etc. Faith quenches these concerns so you can move forward with your life and ministry.

5. The *hope of salvation* (see 1 Thess. 5:8) gives you a confident expectation of victory in every circumstance. It replaces *the defeated "victim mentality" of discouragement and depression* with confidence and courage.

6. *Speaking the Word of God aloud* is an offensive weapon that empowers you to push back the enemy. It takes you from *not knowing how to fight* and gives you a weapon to defend yourself and take new ground for Jesus.

7. *Praying always* with various kinds of prayer is your proactive method of gaining victory without waiting for the enemy to *blindside* you first.

Review

1. How do you defend yourself against lies and deception?
   _____
   _____

2. How do you protect yourself from feelings of unworthiness, guilt, and condemnation?
   _____
   _____

3. What motivates you to quit living for yourself and start living for God?
   _____
   _____

4. How do you deal effectively with troubling thoughts?
   _____
   _____

5. How do you put on the piece of the armor that defends you from discouragement and depression?
   _____
   _____

6. Which weapon do you take when you are in hand-to-hand combat?
   _____
   _____

7. How can you deal with problems at a distance before they are "in your face?"
   _____
   _____

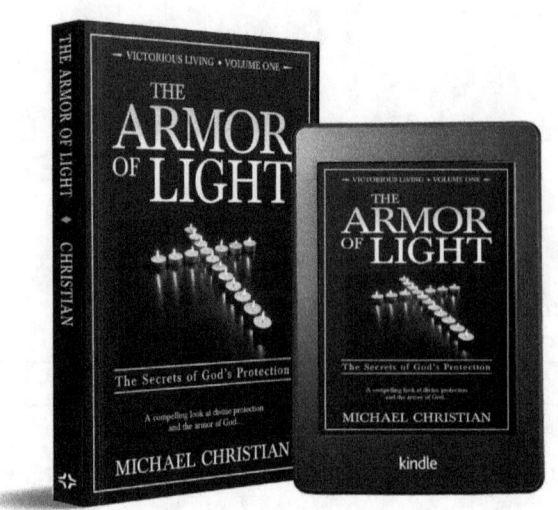

The Armor of Light

The Armor of Light is a high-quality paperback available from https://michaelchristian.us, Amazon.com (paperback and Kindle), Barnes and Noble (paperback and ePub), Apple Books, and fine independent bookstores worldwide.

Volume pricing is available at https://michaelchristian.us for churches, Bible study groups, Sunday School classes, and friends ordering together.

Visit https://michaelchristian.us for additional Bible study resources. A free gift for all readers can be downloaded at https://michaelchristian.us/armor-of-light-resources/.

www.ingramcontent.com/pod-product-compliance
Lightning Source LLC
Chambersburg PA
CBHW060531010526
44110CB00052B/2561